HISTORIC WILLIAMSBURG
A Revolutionary City

by Joanne Mattern

Let's Celebrate America is produced and published by Red Chair Press:
Red Chair Press LLC   PO Box 333   South Egremont, MA 01258-0333
www.redchairpress.com

About the Author

Joanne Mattern is a former editor and the author of nearly 350 books for children and teens. She began writing when she was a little girl and just never stopped! Joanne loves nonfiction because she enjoys bringing history and science topics to life and showing young readers that nonfiction is full of compelling stories! Joanne lives in New York State with her husband, four children, and several pets.

Publisher's Cataloging-In-Publication Data
Names: Mattern, Joanne, 1963–
Title: Historic Williamsburg : a revolutionary city / by Joanne Mattern.

Description: South Egremont, MA : Red Chair Press, [2017] | Series: Let's celebrate America
    | Interest age level: 008-012. | Includes a glossary and references for additional reading.
    | "Core content classroom."--Cover. | Includes bibliographical references and index. |
    Summary: "In the 1770s before the United States was a nation, most people lived on farms.
    But Williamsburg in Virginia Colony was a busy town with wide streets, grand public
    buildings, bustling shops, and a large Market Square. Home to 2,000 people from wealthy
    gentry and middle class shopkeepers to poor slaves. Find out how Colonial Williamsburg
    today gives us a fascinating window into America's past."--Provided by publisher.

Identifiers: LCCN 2016954984 | ISBN 978-1-63440-219-4 (library hardcover) | ISBN 978-1-63440-
    229-3 (paperback) | ISBN 978-1-63440-239-2 (ebook)

Subjects: LCSH: Colonial Williamsburg (Williamsburg, Va.)--Juvenile literature. | United States-
    -History--Colonial period, ca. 1600-1775--Juvenile literature. | Williamsburg (Va.)--History-
    -Revolution, 1775-1783--Juvenile literature. | CYAC: Colonial Williamsburg (Williamsburg,
    Va.) | United States--History--Colonial period, ca. 1600-1775. | Williamsburg (Va.)--History-
    -Revolution, 1775-1783.

Classification: LCC F234.W7 M38 2017 (print) | LCC F234.W7 (ebook) | DDC 975.5/4252--dc23

Map illustration by Joe LeMonnier

Photographs on pages cover, 1, 3, 5, 6, 11, 12, 13, 14, 17, 18, 19, 21, 22, 24, 25, 26, 27, 28, and 29 are used with permission and under license from *The Colonial Williamsburg Foundation*, which is the sole owner of copyright and other proprietary rights in them. However, this is not an official publication of *The Colonial Williamsburg Foundation*, and *The Colonial Williamsburg Foundation* is in no way responsible for the accuracy or any other aspect of the content of this publication.

Photo credits: p. 15: courtesy of William & Mary; p. 4, 20, 30, 31, back cover: Dreamstime; p. 5, 7, 10, 16, 23, 27: Shutterstock

Printed in the United States of America
0517 1P WRZF17

Table of Contents

Step Into the Past

It's a quiet morning in a colonial town in 1775. A farmer passes by on his way to bring his crops to Market Square. Standing in the doorway of her shop, a woman leans on her broom and watches children play marbles on the steps of the church. A slave opens a window onto the street, humming a tune. The sound of marching feet carries through the spring air as soldiers practice their drills in the town square.

Welcome to revolutionary Williamsburg. In this place, the world of 1775 lives on. You can visit this place and see the past brought to life. Today, Williamsburg is a **living history museum** that lets us step back in time and learn what life was like more than two hundred years ago.

At the time of the American Revolution, half of Williamsburg's residents were enslaved Blacks. These slaves worked for white masters, but they had families and traditions of their own. Many new immigrants from Europe came through the bustling city, too. There were even Cherokee boys attending a school to "civilize" them. When courts were in session, the town was busy with people from all across the Virginia colony. The village grew into a bustling center of government, trade, and culture.

In a reenactment, Cherokee are trading with a colonial.

An Important City

During the early 1600s, many people left Great Britain to come to America. In 1607, a group of British men and women settled in the Virginia **colony**. The colony was ruled by Great Britain. It was the first British colony in North America. Jamestown was the first **capital** in the colony.

The Wren Building at the College of William & Mary is the oldest college building in continuous use in the U.S.

Williamsburg grew into another important city in Virginia. Originally a small village called Middle Plantation, it was the home of the College of William & Mary, one of the first colleges in the colonies. Some people thought the site would make a better capital than Jamestown. Students at the College of William & Mary made speeches saying their town should be the capital. Soon, the students got their wish. In 1699, the main government building in Jamestown burned down. Officials agreed to move the capitol building to higher ground instead of rebuilding. The new capital was renamed Williamsburg after King William III of England. The small town quickly grew into a busy center of government, trade, and culture.

It's a Fact

One of the reasons the college students wanted to change the capital was because there were so many mosquitoes in Jamestown! Those mosquitoes spread disease and made life unpleasant.

Williamsburg's Historic Area

1. The Governor's Palace
2. Whythe House
3. The Windmill
4. Bruton Parish Church
5. Randolph House
6. Courthouse
7. Powder Magazine
8. Raleigh Tavern
9. Public Gaol
10. The Capitol

The **modern** city of Williamsburg, Virginia surrounds the restored historic district. The College of William & Mary is two blocks west of the Bruton Parish Church on the edge of the district.

Botetourt St.

A Revolutionary City

In time, the colonists did not want to be part of Great Britain any more. They wanted to be **independent** of the British king's rule. Many of the ideals of democracy were first formed by our nation's leaders in Williamsburg. It was here that the revolutionary Patrick Henry protested unfair taxes from England. Thomas Jefferson studied and practiced law in Williamsburg—and it was here that Jefferson formed his ideas of liberty and freedom that were reflected in his Declaration of Independence. Besides Jefferson, many of the revolution's leaders met here including George Washington, Patrick Henry, James Madison, James Monroe, and many others.

The Declaration of Independence

Patrick Henry once said,
"I know of no way of judging
the future but by the past."

In May 1776, Virginia's representatives, including Washington and George Mason, voted to separate from Great Britain. With this historic vote in Williamsburg, Virginia became the first colony to speak up for independence. But the American colonies had to fight a war with Great Britain before the new nation could be free. Many battles were fought in Virginia. Finally, in 1783, the new United States of America won the war. It was now a free and independent country.

Duke of Gloucester Street, as seen in 1889

By then, Williamsburg was no longer the capital of Virginia. The capital moved to Richmond in 1780. After that, life in Williamsburg got a lot quieter. People still lived and worked there. People still went to the College of William & Mary. However, many people moved away. No one took care of the old colonial houses. The homes and stores began to fall apart. Over the next 100 years, it seemed like revolutionary Williamsburg would be forgotten.

Saving a Town

Bruton Parish Church today.
Inset from early 1900s

One man did not want to see Williamsburg disappear. Reverend Dr. William Archer Rutherfoord Goodwin was the pastor of the Bruton Parish Church in Williamsburg. Goodwin thought it was important to save Williamsburg and its historic buildings. In 1907, he saved his church building in Williamsburg. The church had been built in 1715 and was not in good shape. Goodwin helped find the money to **restore** the church.

In 1908, Goodwin moved to New York. He returned to Williamsburg in 1923 to teach at the College of William & Mary. Goodwin saw that many of the buildings from colonial times were falling apart. He worked with other teachers at the college to save more buildings. But Goodwin did not stop there. He wanted to save the whole town!

The Brafferton is the second-oldest building at the College of William & Mary.

Bruton Parish Church

One of the first buildings of Williamsburg was Bruton Parish Church. The church was an Anglican church. The king was the head of both the Anglican church and the colony. The church and the government ruled the colony together. Taxes were paid to the church.

Each Sunday, everyone was required to attend church by law. The wealthy landowners sat in the front near the pulpit, the shopkeepers and servants sat in the back. Slaves sat in the balcony. This was the only time all social classes gathered in one place.

Inside Bruton Parish Church

Saving a town and restoring buildings costs a lot of money. Goodwin asked many people and organizations to help. Finally, in 1927, he got good news from John D. Rockefeller. Rockefeller started a company called Standard Oil. He was one of the richest men in the United States. Rockefeller and his wife, Abby Aldrich Rockefeller, agreed with Dr. Goodwin that Williamsburg should be restored.

On November 22, 1927, Goodwin shared his big news. He said that Rockefeller would provide the money to restore historic Williamsburg. Rockefeller and Goodwin began buying land. They bought some of the town's oldest homes too. Now it was time to bring the past back to life.

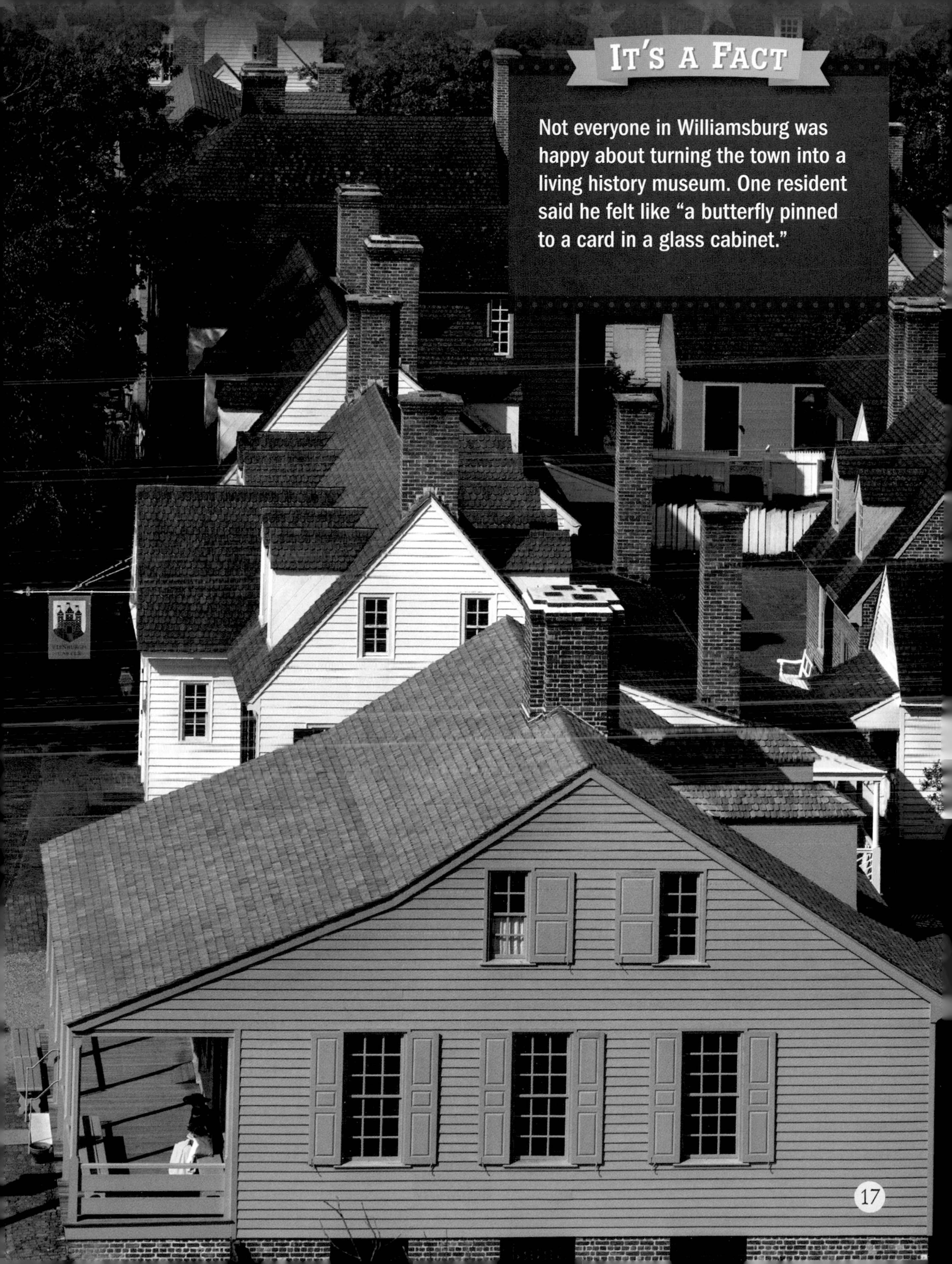

It's a Fact

Not everyone in Williamsburg was happy about turning the town into a living history museum. One resident said he felt like "a butterfly pinned to a card in a glass cabinet."

Making a Museum

It took a lot of work to create old Williamsburg. Goodwin and Rockefeller hired people to study the town. These people checked the buildings. They had to see which buildings should be saved. Some buildings were torn down because they were built after colonial times. Other buildings were in such bad shape they could not be saved.

The workers looked at pictures of the old buildings they saved. They found letters and other documents people had written. These pictures and documents told them what the buildings looked like during colonial times. Then the workers worked to restore or rebuild places so they looked just like they did during the 1700s.

Some of the oldest photos of Williamsburg.
Left to Right: Wythe House, the Courthouse, and Palace Green's Robert Carter House.

The Capitol building was built in the shape of the letter 'H'. One side was for the House of Burgesses and the other side was for the Governor's Council. The section that joined the two sides held the large room where the two houses of government met, called the General Assembly. Members of the House of Burgesses were elected by the landowners of Virginia. They represented the interests of the colonists. The Governor's Council was twelve members appointed by the king. Thy made sure the British laws were obeyed.

The Capitol was first built in 1705. That building burned down. A new Capitol was built in 1740. The Capitol was where Patrick Henry first spoke against King George III of England. When Goodwin and his workers rebuilt the Capitol, they made it look like the original one built in 1705. The restored Capitol opened in 1934.

Duke of Gloucester Street, reconstructed.

For about 30 years, workers restored or rebuilt nearly 500 buildings. Some of these buildings are original. Others were **reconstructed**, or rebuilt, to look like the original. The workers did not just look at homes and businesses. They also restored outhouses and sheds. They made sure everything inside the houses was just like it was in colonial times. Every building was made to look like it had during the 1700s.

The planners also took care to make the area around Williamsburg look like it had during the 1700s. They did not want modern stores in the area. These stores were moved to another part of the town. The planners also made sure no modern highways were built near Williamsburg. They even moved highways away from the town. Today, when visitors drive into historic Williamsburg, they see no modern stores or other businesses.

A Place of Inspiration

Life was difficult during the 1930s. Many people lost their jobs. They lost their homes. Families struggled to stay together. During this time of Great Depression, many people visited Williamsburg. The town was a symbol of how much people struggled during the American Revolution. Williamsburg inspired people to keep working and hoping for better times.

The same was true during the 1940s. From 1939–1945, the world was torn apart by World War II. Williamsburg helped Americans see that their nation could survive during war. America could come out of the hard times stronger than ever.

Soldiers pose on a World War I tank on Duke of Gloucester Street.

The Governors Palace was reconstructed on the original site after a fire destroyed it in 1781.

Rockefeller and his team worked hard to make sure historic Williamsburg was a great place to visit. A Visitors Center was built. Buses brought people from the Visitors Center into the historic district. People came from all over the nation to explore the past.

Times Change

Old Williamsburg presented a lot of history. However, only some stories were told. Most of the stories were about rich white men who made history. Visitors did not hear much about women or Native Americans. They did not hear what life was like for servants or poor people. Most of all, they did not hear about slavery.

There were slaves in Williamsburg during colonial times. However, their stories were not told at the museum. The restored Williamsburg did not explain what life was really like for slaves and their families.

Slaves return from working in the fields.

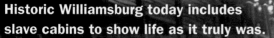

Historic Williamsburg today includes slave cabins to show life as it truly was.

Things began to change in 1977. Historic Williamsburg decided to tell different stories than it had in the past. The museum put on special programs about women and slaves. Finally, in 1988, slave cabins were reconstructed near Williamsburg. Slaves became part of the town, just as they had been 200 years earlier. Free black men and women were also added to the story.

Today, visitors can walk the streets of revolutionary Williamsburg and feel like they are living in the 1700s. Every building is historically accurate. Visitors can go into homes and shops and see what life was like over 200 years ago. They can argue with Patrick Henry or eat a meal with Thomas Jefferson.

Buildings are an important part of historic Williamsburg. However, they do not tell the whole story. The most important part of the town is its people. The people who work in old Williamsburg try to be just like the people who lived there in colonial times. These people are called **interpreters**. They dress in colonial clothes. They speak like people did in Williamsburg in colonial times. They do colonial jobs the same way they were done in the 1700s.

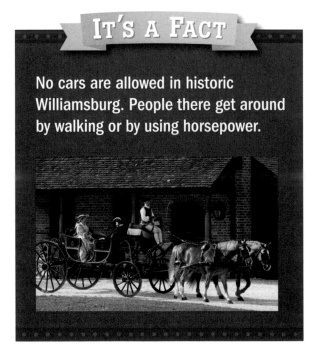

IT'S A FACT

No cars are allowed in historic Williamsburg. People there get around by walking or by using horsepower.

Interpreters acting out a colonial times scene.

Visitors can watch the interpreters do their jobs. They can see how people worked and played. They can see what people ate and how they spent their time.

Interpreters also act out scenes or plays that show what life was like in colonial times. They act out the events that people were talking about between 1774 and 1781. Interpreters act out political arguments and meetings. They talk about social events that were important during that time.

The British Army entering the city.

The buildings and streets in Williamsburg are used as **sets** for these events. Visiting is like watching a play. Only this play is not taking place on a stage. This play is taking place all around you!

Sometimes the interpreters in historic Williamsburg show what life was like on ordinary days. Other times, there are special themes. For example, the town might be buzzing because George Washington is coming for a visit. Or people might be worried because the British army is marching close to town. No matter what the theme, the interpreters play their parts. They act just like people probably did during the 1770s.

Each year, thousands of visitors walk the streets of old Williamsburg. They are able to get an up-close view of life during the 1700s. However, Williamsburg is much more than just a living history museum.

Historic Williamsburg can also help us understand how our own lives are connected to the lives of those who lived in the past. By walking its streets or viewing its programs, we can see that some things are very much the same now as then. We may live in a very different world and have very different customs. But deep down, we face the same fears and joys as people did more than two hundred years ago. These common themes help us understand what it means to be an American, no matter what the date is.

Interpreters dressed as George and Martha Washington.

Glossary

capital: a city that is the seat of government

colony: a country or area that is under the control of another nation

independent: free from outside control

interpreters: people who act out or explain historical events

living history museum: a museum that recreates historical settings so visitors can experience the past first-hand

modern: having to do with the present time

reconstructed: rebuilt to look like the original

restore: to repair a building so it returns to its original condition

sets: buildings that are used in a play or performance

Learn More in the Library

Books

Brenner, Barbara. *If You Lived in Williamsburg in Colonial Days.* Scholastic, 2000.

Kalman, Bobbie. *A Colonial Town: Williamsburg (Historic Communities).* Crabtree Publishing, 1992.

Kostyal, K.M. *1776: A New Look at Revolutionary Williamsburg.* National Geographic Children's Books, 2009.

Web Site

The Colonial Williamsburg Foundation

www.colonialwilliamsburg.org

Index